Motivation
and
Mental
Toughness

© The National Coaching Foundation, 2005
Reprinted 2002, 2003 © sports coach UK

First published 1996, reprinted 1999, 2001
© The National Coaching Foundation

sports coach UK is the brand name of The National Coaching Foundation and has been such since April 2001.

ISBN-13: 978-1-902523-24-5
ISBN-10: 1-902523-24-5

Editors
Phil Cabral and Penny Crisfield

Sub-editors
Fiona Carpenter, Rosie Connell, Jake Downey
John Honeybourne, Terry McMorris, Mark Nesti
Lloyd Readhead and Andy Smith

Typesetter
Debbie Backhouse

Cover photo courtesy of actionplus sports images.

sports coach UK would like to thank Chris Sellars and Auriel Forrester
for their valuable input to the 2003 reprint

Coachwise Business Solutions

sports coach UK
114 Cardigan Road
Headingley
Leeds LS6 3BJ
Tel: 0113-274 4802
Fax: 0113-275 5019
Email: coaching@sportscoachuk.org
Website: www.sportscoachuk.org

Patron: HRH The Princess Royal

Published on behalf of **sports coach UK** by
Coachwise Business Solutions
Coachwise Ltd
Chelsea Close
Off Amberley Road
Armley
Leeds LS12 4HP
Tel: 0113-231 1310
Fax: 0113-231 9606
Email: enquiries@coachwisesolutions.co.uk
Website: www.coachwisesolutions.co.uk

Why do some performers respond better under the stress of competition than others? How do good performers prepare for competition? How do some coaches consistently develop successful teams? How can sport psychology help coaches and performers? These are just some of the questions asked by sports performers and coaches.

This new handbook is for coaches, performers, teachers and students who want to find the answers to these and other questions. Based on sound psychological principles[1], it is written in an easy to read style and uncluttered by unnecessary jargon. It provides a wealth of practical advice, with panels showing how the information and ideas can be directly applied to coaching practice.

The resource explains how to:

- increase and sustain motivation (Chapter One)
- balance the needs of the individual with those of the team or squad (Chapter One)
- develop mental toughness by using mental skills to improve concentration, confidence, commitment and emotional control (Chapter Two).

1   This resource does not cover the skill learning aspect of sport psychology. For information in this area, you are recommended to the **scUK** workshop *Improving Practices and Skill* and its accompanying resource (complimentary with the workshop or available from Coachwise 1st4sport on 0113-201 5555 or via www.1st4sport.com).

Every chapter includes tasks and information panels to help relate the text to sports practice, and summary panels to highlight and reinforce the main points. Each chapter concludes with references and tasks for those who wish to apply the knowledge to their own practice and/or generate evidence towards vocational qualifications.

Throughout this pack, the pronouns he, she, him, her and so on are interchangeable and intended to be inclusive of both males and females. It is important in sport, as elsewhere, that both genders have equal status and opportunities.

Contents

CHAPTER ONE:
Motivation and Performance

1.0 Introduction

Some coaches believe that motivation is simply about psyching-up performers but human behaviour is not so simple. Most performers have a number of reasons or motives for participating in sport, which often change over time. For example, performers may initially join a group for social reasons but later might wish to improve their skill level. Some common motives for participating in sport include to:

- have fun
- make friends
- find adventure and excitement
- improve health and fitness
- achieve success or win
- be selected for a representative team
- learn new techniques and develop skill.

These are general motives and performers will have their own particular reasons for participating based on their personal needs, aims and ambitions. Coaches should strive to understand each performer's personal motives because they affect performance significantly.

Personal motives encourage performers to:

- train and improve
- learn, develop and apply themselves to overcome opponents in competitive situations
- work together as a team.

Highly motivated performers are those who know what they are trying to achieve and strive to achieve their goals when the opportunity arises. The challenge is for coaches to help performers identify and use their personal motives to improve and achieve success. This task is not easy, particularly with young performers who may not know what they are trying to achieve.

sports coach UK

The nature of the environment in which coaching takes place can also significantly affect a performer's motivation (eg friendly, supportive, positive). Creating an appropriate environment in which performers achieve success is also a challenge for coaches. To help performers achieve success, coaches need to:

- discuss with each of their performers, their needs, aims and ambitions (ie establish personal motives), set and monitor goals, and nurture the performer's own self-motivation

- enhance motivation by designing stimulating and challenging practices and sessions

- create an open, friendly and motivating environment in which performers achieve success and enjoy sport.

1.1 Establishing Personal Motives

The term **motivation** refers to the reason why people choose to do some things, the manner in which they choose to do them (ie characteristic way) and why they avoid doing other things (ie why they approach certain situations or actions and avoid others). Personal motivation stems from both:

- inside the performer – usually referred to as **intrinsic** or self-motivation (eg for self-satisfaction, achievement)

- outside the performer – usually referred to as **extrinsic** (eg for external rewards).

Coaches need to be aware of the various motives that influence each performer at any one time and they should tailor their coaching accordingly. To do this, they need to develop a good working relationship with performers and their parents, families, friends and teachers (ie those who have a significant impact on the performer). In this way, they will be able to establish the dominant motives by:

- asking performers what they like/dislike and what motivates them

- asking each performer's family members what the performer likes/dislikes

- watching performers during training and competition to see what they appear to enjoy and dislike.

To develop these relationships, coaches need effective communication skills. These skills enable coaches to create an open but dynamic and interactive environment, in which performers are encouraged to ask questions and try out new and different ideas without the fear of being ridiculed or put down. This is not easy but is essential to good coaching.

TASK

How can you tell when one of your performers is highly motivated?

What makes you think a performer's motivation is low?

How and when do you notice any changes in the individual?

Think of a highly motivated performer in your sport.

Try to establish why the performer has a high level of motivation and how she maintains it.

How might you foster this motivation?

Repeat this exercise with a performer who seems to lack motivation.

Carrying out this exercise will help you find ways to nurture each performer's motivation.

Two performers might be striving to achieve the same goal (eg run 100m in 11secs). However, their motivation for achieving the goal may be different

– one may be striving to prove himself and seek public recognition by being the fastest in the club, the other may be trying to achieve his best by setting a short-term goal to run 100m in 10.5secs. Although they may have the same goals, performers rarely have the same motives because of their different backgrounds, experiences and abilities. Psychologists have put forward theories in an attempt to account for differences in motivation. These theories are based on factors within both the:

- performer (eg personal needs, expectations, personality)
- situation in which the performance is taking place (eg rewards, coach's behaviour).

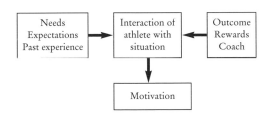

Figure 1: The interaction model of motivation

The research suggests that to understand motivation, it is important to consider the interaction between the performer and the situation. The model on the previous page (Figure 1) explains why:

- two individuals may behave differently in the same situation

- the same individual may behave differently in different situations (eg low motivation in practice, high motivation in competitions)

- an individual may behave differently in the same situation on different occasions.

The differences in motivation between performers may be the result of their goals – they are striving to achieve different outcomes from activities. This is sometimes referred to as having different **goal orientations** – some performers may view sport as an opportunity to:

- demonstrate their personal ability or mastery of a skill or task (ie mastery orientation)

- display their superiority or satisfy their ego (ie ego orientation)

- gain social approval (ie social approval orientation).

Performers with a **mastery orientation** view success as trying new techniques and challenges, and overcoming problems.

Ego-oriented performers view success as winning and having superior ability.

Social-approval-oriented performers view success as receiving praise from others, meeting people and developing friendships.

Performers often possess combinations of these orientations and switch from one to another at various times.

Young performers' personal motives and goal orientation will probably vary as they develop and according to their involvement in sport. Young performers use information from a variety of sources to build a picture of themselves. The views of others can be important (ie gaining social approval) to their self-image. Coaches need to be sensitive to the orientations of young performers so they help them to maintain and enhance their motivation for sport.

TASK

Which of the three categories of orientations (ie mastery, ego, social approval) seem to represent most strongly your motivation for sport?

Do you think that having the same view of success is important for the coach and performer?

Consider the situation of helping to maintain the motivation of a mastery-oriented performer and an ego-oriented performer in training and competition. How would you structure training sessions to cater for these two performers?

1.2 Enhancing Motivation

Many achievements in competition occur as a result of improvements gained through training. If performers do not possess the intrinsic (ie internal) motivation to improve their performance in training, their ability to learn and develop will suffer and their performance will not improve. Motivation for training is as important as in competition. Through an understanding of each performer's personal motives, coaches can structure practices, sessions and the coaching environment to help performers to learn, refine and apply

their skills efficiently and successfully. Coaches can enhance motivation in training and competition by:

- effective goal setting
- giving rewards
- their coaching behaviour (eg how they structure sessions, communicate with performers, and involve them in their own development).

Each will be considered in subsequent sections.

1.3 Goal Setting

This is one of the most important coaching tools, because it can give performers direction and help them to achieve success. Through goal setting, coaches can help performers to learn new techniques and develop skill. The successful attainment of these goals will in turn help to increase motivation and self-confidence, focus attention and reduce anxiety. Coaches and performers need to discuss and agree goals which should be based on each performer's needs and ambitions. These needs and ambitions should form each performer's long-term goals. From these, the process of effective goal setting will help to identify intermediate and short-term goals to map out a path to achieve the long-term goals.

The way goals are set and the type of goals set is crucial if performers are to achieve their long-term goals. Society places a strong emphasis on winning. This has resulted in many performers (especially the young) equating winning with success and losing with failure. Modifying this view is important so all performers, no matter whether they win or lose, achieve some success during their training and competition. Success helps performers develop and maintain self-confidence[1]. The more success performers experience in certain behaviours or situations, the greater their self-confidence in that behaviour or situation. Encouraging performers to focus on personal achievement rather than winning, gives them greater control and confidence in their ability to influence the likelihood of success.

It may help to differentiate two types of goals: **outcome** and **process** goals. While long-term goals may often describe a particular **outcome** (eg winning a medal, gaining selection), performers should focus their intermediate and short-term goals more frequently on **process** goals (eg achieving a certain time/ distance, reducing the number of unforced errors, increasing the number of successful attempts at beating a defender). This is because process goals, unlike outcome goals, are more directly under the performer's control (ie you can control your own performance but not that of the opposition). Outcome goals are never totally under the control of the individual – you can achieve a personal best, perform exceptionally well but still fail to win or gain selection because another competitor performs better.

It is easier to set process goals in individual sports such as swimming or athletics, for these normally relate to improvements in times and distances. However, with some imagination it is also possible to set process goals in games such as hockey or cricket (see Table 1). Performers and coaches should set SMART process goals which are more likely to offer performers success, which in turn increases self-confidence and motivation.

---

1   For more details on self-confidence see Section 2.2, Page 38.

Principles of goal setting

S pecific	Should be as specific as possible to focus attention
M easurable	To assess progress against a standard
A greed	By both the performer and coach
R ealistic	Challenging and achievable within the performer's capability
T ime phased	With a specific date for completion

Table 1: Example of SMART training goals

	Hockey	Cricket	Athletics
Specific	To beat a defender on the open stick side	To play a front foot cover drive which hits the boundary	To run 400m in 58 seconds
Measurable	Ten repetitions	Twenty repetitions	Over five runs
Agreed	Yes	Yes	Yes
Realistic	60% success rate	70% success rate	80% success rate
Time Phased	30 December	1 August	1 June

TASK

Try to identify typical outcome goals in your sport. Then devise a number of process goals that are under the performer's control. Process goals are more likely to produce success which will enhance motivation towards the attainment of the long-term goals. You may notice that carefully set process goals often lead to the attainment of the outcome goal.

Involving the Performer

It is important to involve performers in setting their own long- and short-term goals. This is far more motivating and helps them to feel in control of their destiny. The goals must be clear, achievable and agreed by the performer and coach (ie SMART). For example, a marathon runner may feel that achieving second place in a race is unrealistic (ie an outcome goal). However, revising the goal so it is under the runner's control helps to maintain the runner's intrinsic motivation (eg completing the race in less than three hours which is a process goal). It also helps to ensure the runner successfully achieves the goal.

1.4 Rewards

Coaches often use rewards to enhance motivation. A large number and wide variety of rewards are commonly in use in sport:

- extrinsic rewards such as trophies, overseas trips, money and kit.
- intrinsic rewards such as self-satisfaction, feelings of competence, enjoyment and achievement.

Rewards can also be tangible (eg trophies, medals, colours, money, representative trips) – these are quantifiable and visible. Intangible rewards (eg praise, publicity, parental satisfaction, friendships, approval from peers) are more difficult to quantify as they are not in a material form. Although rewards can be powerful motivators, they should be used with some caution, for research shows they do not always increase motivation. The effect of rewards depends on the motivational orientation (eg mastery, ego, social approval) of the individual. Coaches, performers and other significant individuals (eg parents, friends) who continually emphasise winning and gaining rewards, can influence performers (particularly the young) to participate solely for the rewards and not also for the intrinsic experience of achieving success.

Extrinsic and Intrinsic Rewards

To be effective, rewards should provide performers with information to improve or reinforce their performance and enhance intrinsic motivation. Performers with high intrinsic motivation have the desire to improve and achieve success (eg praise can encourage a performer to try again at a personal best or new skill). It is important for all involved in sport to understand the advantages and disadvantages of rewards because they affect performers in a variety of ways. The following panels give you some insight about the value and impact of extrinsic rewards.

In the cartoon, the man is trying to cajole the donkey into running the race but the donkey does not want to move. The man dangles a carrot in front of the donkey to encourage it to walk forward. Still no success. He stands behind the donkey with a stick in his hand and tries beating it to make it move forward. The donkey moves but the movement is to kick the man in the leg.

The carrot had no effect because the donkey was not hungry. Beating the donkey made the donkey move but not in the way the man wanted.

To help performers achieve their goals, coaches need to nurture the hunger in their performers and offer them appropriate rewards.

A young squash player was competing in a local league. The player gained intrinsic motivation though enjoyment and self-satisfaction. As the player's skill level improved so did the league results which led to regular extrinsic rewards (eg medals, trophies). As the player became more competent, she began to associate squash with winning and receiving rewards. Unfortunately, the winning and rewards began to replace the player's original intrinsic motivation.

As time passed, the player entered a higher league. Although the skill level continued to improve, the player experienced feelings of incompetence when losing to better players. She gradually stopped winning and began to lose the motivation provided by the medals and the associated feelings of self-satisfaction. Finally, the squash player gave up and returned to the local league in an attempt to regain the feelings of competence, achievement, satisfaction and enjoyment.

Coaches need to ensure that extrinsic rewards do not become so important that the intrinsic value of the activity is lost, and the performer's motivation suffers.

Young boys were playing football outside an old man's house. The old man did not like the noise the boys were making but he was not sure how to get rid of them. Then he struck upon an idea. While the boys were playing, he went outside and gave each one 50p. The boys were overjoyed because someone was paying them to play football, so they came back the next day. Sure enough, the old man came out to see them but this time he only gave each boy 30p. On the third day the old man only gave the boys 10p. The boys were frustrated and could not understand why they only received 10p when they originally received 50p. In the end they thought it was not worth their while so they decided to pack up and play somewhere else.

The original intrinsic motivation for playing football was replaced by the extrinsic motivation of the money. When the extrinsic motivation was removed, so was the desire to continue playing football. Intrinsic motivation is important for achieving long-term goals; rewards should be carefully chosen otherwise they may alter a performer's intrinsic motivation.

Think of a reward you have previously received.

Why were you given the reward?

Did the reward give you any information about your performance?

Did it affect your subsequent motivation or performance?

Competence, Control and Responsibility

Intrinsically motivated performers do not need to receive extrinsic rewards to motivate them to participate (eg a tennis player who looks forward to a match, a swimmer who enjoys the challenge of a competition). These performers play sport for pleasure and to achieve success, though they may also have other external motives and incentives for participating.

If extrinsic rewards are to boost motivation effectively, they should always provide information about ability and competence (eg an extrinsic reward offered to the player who makes the greatest improvement in a skill test). Their use should not be for controlling or forcing changes in behaviour (eg rewards for arriving at training on time). Similarly, if rewards (or the lack of them) inform performers that they are incompetent, the performers' intrinsic motivation will decrease. For example, if a gymnastic coach rewards a gymnast for completing a somersault but this action does not usually receive a reward when the performance is by a more able gymnast, the gymnast may perceive the reward as in indication of a lack of ability. As a result he may have a lower motivation to continue competing in gymnastics.

However, rewards are generally found to be more effective than punishments (eg it is better to reward those who improve on the shuttle run drill than to punish those who come last or fail to improve).

Coaches should generally try to find ways to enhance intrinsic motivation rather than rely on the short-term benefits of extrinsic rewards. Performers develop greater intrinsic motivation if they feel they are in control and are encouraged to accept personal responsibility for their performances. Extrinsic rewards tend not to encourage personal responsibility and can therefore be viewed as controlling behaviour.

Coaches should nurture their performers' intrinsic motivation so they are less reliant on external rewards that may not always be present. The only way to decide the effectiveness of rewards is to know your performers (ie their goal orientations) and understand what motivates them. Knowing what motivates each performer defines the appropriate reward for that individual.

SUMMARY

To be effective, rewards should:

- provide information which reinforces the performer's feelings of competence.

Rewards should not:

- be used to control or force changes in behaviour.

1.5 Your Coaching Behaviour

The way you involve performers in their own development, structure sessions, communicate and provide feedback can all have a significant impact on the motivation of your performers.

Involving Performers

To enhance intrinsic motivation, performers should be encouraged to take responsibility for their own behaviour and the outcomes of their performance. This is achieved by involving performers in the design and running of their own training and competitions. In many situations, coaches can plan training and competition programmes in conjunction with performers or more experienced members of the team or squad. Most performers can also be encouraged to help plan coaching or training sessions (or parts of them) and perhaps help run different parts of the session (eg to take the warm-up, or demonstrate a particular move). Some performers may be able to contribute to decision making (eg which competitions to enter, who to select, which strategies to use).

In this way, performers can take more responsibility for their own performance. Improvements and success can also be more readily attributed to their efforts and involvement (see Page 22). Therefore, intrinsic motivation is raised. Coaches should give extrinsic rewards carefully and should actively encourage performers to contribute to the planning, organisation, decision making and leading of coaching programmes and sessions.

How often do you involve your performers in planning and decision making?

Can you think of any occasions when you could do this?

How often do you encourage your performers to lead different parts of the session?

How can you encourage your performers to take more responsibility for their behaviour?

Structuring Sessions

The way coaching and training sessions are structured can influence the motivation level of the performers. In addition to encouraging performers to be involved in the planning and delivery of sessions where appropriate, coaches need to think about variety in their sessions. The same warm-up, the same drills or even the same session format, however effective, will become boring over time.

Coaches need to be innovative and design sessions that are effective but interesting, balancing the need for repetition and reinforcement with the desire for originality and fresh ideas.

Remember too that all performers are different – they have their unique likes and dislikes, their own goals and motivations; variety in sessions is more likely to appeal to each performer at some point.

TASK

Consider the following example. Two footballers play for the same team and follow the same training programme. One enjoys competing to achieve success, he hates losing and continually seeks praise from his team-mates. The other participates for fun and to get better. As a coach, how would you structure coaching sessions to cater for these individuals?

Communication and Behaviour

Clear and effective communication between coach and performer is a key factor influencing motivation. Good communication is needed to discuss and agree goals, inspire performers to strive for these goals, provide positive and constructive feedback, nurture self-confidence and empower performers to be responsible for their own performance and behaviour. The principles of effective communication are summarised in the panel on the following page.

Effective communication in coaching involves:

- good listening skills
- gaining attention before giving information
- providing concise information using clear, simple statements
- good use of the voice (eg pitch, resonance, tone, volume, variety)
- reading non-verbal messages
- maintaining a positive manner
- possessing an extensive knowledge of the sport and performers so coaches can talk to individuals using appropriate terminology.

In addition to communication, the coaching style adopted by coaches can significantly affect motivation. Coaches tend to have a preferred coaching style. Styles range along a continuum from a performer-centred approach to a coach-centred one (see Figure 2).

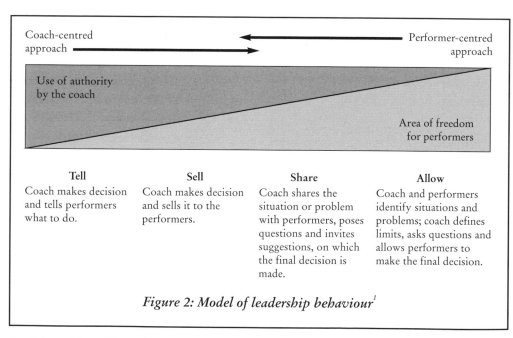

Tell	Sell	Share	Allow
Coach makes decision and tells performers what to do.	Coach makes decision and sells it to the performers.	Coach shares the situation or problem with performers, poses questions and invites suggestions, on which the final decision is made.	Coach and performers identify situations and problems; coach defines limits, asks questions and allows performers to make the final decision.

Figure 2: Model of leadership behaviour[1]

1   Adapted from Tennenbaum and Schmidt's 1973 model of leadership behaviour.

Typically coaches use a combination of **telling** (giving information), **showing** (using demonstrations) and **asking** (questioning) when coaching performers. No one style is necessarily right or wrong – each has a place in a particular situation or with a certain performer. However, good coaches should develop a range of styles beyond their preferred or most comfortable, so they can select the most appropriate style for the individual or group, or to suit a particular situation.

TASK

Think about the styles of coaching you use and compare them with a successful coach you have observed. How do they differ?

Do you always use the same coaching style in every situation?

Would one style be more effective with a particular performer or group of performers?

How effective would a telling style be at enhancing motivation prior to a competition?

What might be the impact of this style on motivation following a competition?

To promote intrinsic motivation, coaches need to be careful not to rely too heavily on a telling style – it has an important place but not when setting goals or encouraging self-responsibility and involvement. In these situations questioning can be the more effective style.

The panel on the next page provides further guidance about the behaviour and communication styles that young performers like and dislike in their coaches.

For more information you are recommended to the **scUK** workshop *Coaching Children and Young People* and the resource *Coaching Young Performers* (complimentary with the workshop or available from Coachwise 1st4sport on 0113 201 5555 or via www.1st4sport.com).

Children like coaches who:

- are friendly, happy, patient, understanding and have a sense of humour
- have credibility in the sport
- are firm but fair
- provide encouragement when it is due
- are well organised
- help them develop their skills.

Children do not like coaches who:

- shout
- constantly say 'well done', no matter the effort or skill displayed
- appear indecisive[1].

Feedback

Feedback can significantly affect performance and motivation depending on how it is presented. Coaches should give feedback so it is non-threatening. Performers who are comfortable receiving feedback are generally more receptive to new ideas. Feedback can be:

- positive, where performers receive praise and/or rewards for successful aspects of performance and this encourages them to feel competent and self-confident
- negative, where the emphasis is on errors and results in performers feeling incompetent and low in self-confidence.

Performers who receive positive feedback tend to enjoy sport, show enthusiasm and maintain motivation to continue participating. The content and method of delivery of any negative or corrective points should address the area of weakness but maintain intrinsic motivation.

Negative feedback should also be aimed at the behaviour and not at the performer (ie 'your fitness level is below the standard' rather than 'you are not up to the standard').

1   Younger children tend not to want to be included in decision making but prefer to trust the coach to make the right decisions. As they grow older, they want and should be encouraged to take more responsibility.

The most appropriate way of giving corrective feedback is through the burger approach (Figure 3). The filling represents the corrective feedback and the bun represents the positive praise on either side of the correction (ie praise followed by the corrective feedback followed by further praise).

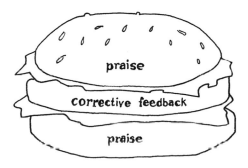

Figure 3: The praise burger

TASK

A gymnast may complete a floor exercise but make one mistake in a tumbling routine. The emphasis of the corrective feedback should be on improving the floor routine and the tumbling error. How would you maintain the performer's motivation and correct the errors simultaneously?

1.6 Problems with Motivation

Inevitably, individuals will suffer peaks and troughs in their level of motivation. It is the coach's role to be receptive to these fluctuations and to recognise the typical factors that are likely to affect motivation adversely. Two groups of factors are considered in this section:

- Adherence and Overtraining
- Progress and Setbacks

Adherence and Overtraining

Well-designed coaching programmes help performers improve and become more skilful in the most efficient and effective manner. However, they are only effective if performers are happy to follow them. Research suggests performers adhere either too little or too much. Certain factors influence a performer's adherence:

- a good understanding of the programme's goals
- finding sessions challenging and stimulating
- appropriately structured competition
- enjoyable and friendly atmosphere where performers are made to feel welcome.

Other factors may influence a performer's **non-adherence** to a coaching programme:

- not understanding the programme's goals
- finding the sessions boring, too hard or too easy
- too competitive/not competitive enough
- too serious and with a lack of enjoyment
- injury or fear of injuries
- friends dropping out
- conflicting pressures of work, school, family or other sports
- distraction of other interests.

The following factors can contribute to **overtraining** or over adherence:

- excessive peer, coach, family or self-generated pressure to succeed
- failure to understand the programme/not achieving goals
- enjoyment and social attraction
- lack of other interests
- too much spare time.

For coaches, understanding a performer's motives for participating is the starting point for encouraging adherence and recognising the possibility of over-adherence or overtraining. These motives, however, can change over time particularly if the performer is young. Coaches need to be aware and sensitive to these changes and should work with performers to amend the programmes accordingly.

Intrinsic motivation (see Section 1.1, Page 2) can help to predict adherence – performers with high intrinsic motivation adhere to training programmes better than those with low intrinsic motivation. The research suggests that other interests that conflict with sport are the main reason for non-adherence (eg family, other sports, work, school). Therefore, when planning competition and training programmes, coaches and performers should work together to devise a self-motivating programme. However, they should consider outside interests that may limit a performer's commitment to the programme. Coaches can help performers adhere more closely to training programmes by:

- explaining clearly what they are doing and why they are doing it
- giving performers positive experiences and regular success
- recording the success and feeding the information back to performers regularly.

TASK

If you are a coach, ask one of your performers the following questions, or if you are a performer, ask yourself:

Why do you participate in sport?

Why do you participate in this sport?

What do you hope to achieve from this sport?

Are you as keen to participate now as you were when you originally started?

If no, why not?

If yes, what do you think helps you to remain so keen?

How can the coach help you to develop and/or maintain your motivation and enthusiasm for this sport?

These questions will enable you to gain a good insight into some motives for participating. Coaches should repeat this exercise with every performer to obtain a clear picture of each performer's motives for competing in sport.

Progress and Setbacks

Unscheduled breaks in training occur no matter how good the structure of training programmes (eg due to injury, illness). The breaks can adversely affect motivation because the delays in progress may mean performers are not able to achieve their goal. In cases where a setback results in a loss of physical conditioning, performers may feel that the attainment of their previous level is too demanding. Revising goals to take account of the delay or setback can help performers regain their physical conditioning and motivate them to return to their sport.

Coaches and performers can use a variety of techniques to maintain motivation and adherence during the retraining process. These include:

- mental rehearsal which enables passive practice of techniques or rehearsal of strategies

- relaxation and imagery to deal with anxiety that performers may experience due to the injury

- verbal persuasion to help motivation and to replace negative, irrational thoughts about the sport, themselves and the injury

- social support to talk through problems and support each other (eg pairing an injured performer with another performer who has overcome injury or establishing an injury support group).

When setbacks occur, reassessing and adjusting goals is essential to maintain progress with all performers. However, this is particularly important with injured performers where a goal-setting rehabilitation programme can limit the loss of physical conditioning. Injured performers require specific support to maintain their motivation. Performers should be involved in all aspects of the sport to help them maintain motivation.

For example, when a canoeist suffered a shoulder injury and became temporarily unable to paddle, the coach and performer had to reassess the season's goals to allow adequate time for recovery and successful rehabilitation.

The coach encouraged the canoeist to become involved in other aspects of training (eg land-based training, and assisting with the planning of training sessions for other canoeists). This helped the canoeist to maintain the motivation to recover and achieve the goal of successful rehabilitation.

1.7 Motivation and Competition

Coaches and performers need to plan the preparation to reach the day/start of competition with optimal motivation in terms of direction and intensity. They can then be secure in the knowledge that the performer is well prepared and motivated to achieve the agreed goal.

Before Competition

Some time before the event the coach needs to find out each performer's technical, physical, tactical and mental condition. Then the coach needs to design practices and sessions that motivate performers to reach the standard required for competition. In the build up to the event, coaches need to provide simulated competitive experiences that allow performers to become familiar and sensitised to the competitive situation, and confident in their ability. This helps performers to maintain their confidence, motivation and focus on the goal for competition.

A performer's confidence may vary as competition approaches. Knowing how to help performers remain focused and motivated prior to competition is often difficult for coaches. Too much, too little or information given at the wrong time can make performers anxious. The coach's knowledge of each performer can be invaluable in knowing what to say and when to say it. Encouraging performers to use verbal persuasion may help them to strive for their goals (refer to Section 2.5, Page 56); visualization or imagery may help to reassure them of their ability.

If performers perceive themselves as unable to achieve their goals, they are less likely to approach the competition with high levels of motivation. A goal that is achievable 70% of the time in training, may only be achieved 40% of the time in competition because of the added pressures associated with competition. This is especially true if performers are ego-oriented and place a high emphasis on showing superior ability.

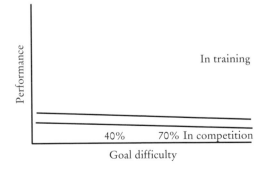

Figure 4: Influence of anxiety on goal difficulty

During Competition

Performers should be encouraged to take responsibility for their own performance and not become too reliant on the coach during the competition. The rules of some sports do not permit any interaction by the coach – the performer is forced to take responsibility. However, in others the coach may have a direct opportunity to influence a performer's motivation (eg during half-time, time outs, between heats/events).

Performers who focus on the outcome of the event for achieving success can gain valuable information about their progress. However, too much emphasis on the outcome of competition can lead a performer to compete merely for victory and extrinsic rewards and not intrinsic or personal satisfaction. Performers who focus on the outcome, and who do not regularly achieve victory or receive extrinsic rewards, will soon lose self-confidence and the motivation to strive for success. Performers should set specific goals that allow them to experience success more than failure. Focusing on agreed process goals, over which they have greater control, can help performers experience success and enhance their motivation.

Attributing Success and Failure

If performers use process goals to achieve success, after the event they can confidently attribute the successful attainment of the goal to their own action. This is because they have retained control over their success. For example, after the 1996 Olympic 400m final, Roger Black was pleased to achieve a silver medal and attributed his success to the fact that he set a goal of running his own race and achieved it. His personal success was achieved irrespective of how the opposition performed. His intrinsic reward was personal satisfaction; his extrinsic reward was a silver medal. If a performer fails to achieve a goal, the performer and coach should reassess the goal to determine the reason and whether or not it was realistic.

Failures in training provide valuable information which gives performers opportunities to learn from their mistakes. However, failures in competition can be detrimental to self-confidence, particularly with young performers. Therefore, performers and coaches should adjust competition goals to take account of the pressures and yet still enable performers to achieve success.

Progress can be achieved in competition by resetting the goal after each competition (ie if successful, increase the difficulty; if unsuccessful, decrease the difficulty).

Performers who set outcome goals cannot directly control their success. Therefore they cannot have confidence in their ability to change the situation. This can lead to an increase in anxiety and worry (see Section 2.4, Page 48) and subsequently a poor performance. This underlines the importance of coaches knowing the performers well and understanding their motivational orientation to help them set competition goals that are meaningful, realistic and appropriate. Shortly after the event, coaches and performers should determine the achievements and evaluate the success of the goals. Then they should reset the goals for the next period of coaching and competition.

The outcome of competition is not the only factor to affect motivation (eg win or lose). A subjective appraisal of performance ('I won, but I didn't perform well') and the explanation given by the performer ('OK, I performed well today. However, my opponent wasn't very good') can affect motivation.

Performers generally attribute success and failure (see Figure 5) according to whether or not the:

- factors were constant (ie stable) or variable (ie unstable)

- outcome was attributed to their own behaviour (internal) or to the behaviour of others or the situation (external).

- factors were under their control[1].

If performers attribute the outcome of their actions to external factors (eg 'I was lucky to get away with that one; that was a hard game'), they feel they have little control over those factors. If they attribute the outcomes to factors within their control (eg 'I hit my forehands really well; I worked hard to win every point'), they believe in their ability to influence the outcome. Coaches who are aware of how performers attribute success and failure can help them take greater responsibility for their actions, and increase self-confidence and motivation towards achieving their goals.

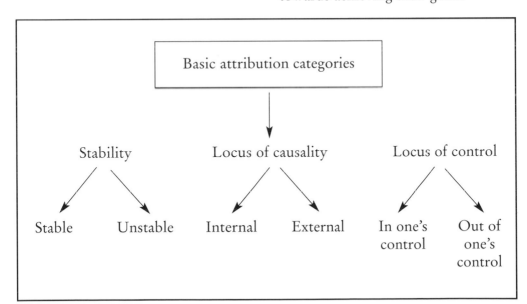

Figure 5: Model of attributions

1   Weiner, B. (1972) *Theories of Motivation: From Mechanism to Cognition.* Chicago: Markham. ISBN: 0-528620-18-5.

For example, in a relay race (eg athletics, swimming), certain team members may respond to losing a race by training harder, being self-critical and committing themselves to improving the performance of the team and themselves. Others may feel that a specific team member is responsible for the result which could decrease team motivation and cause conflict between members.

Coaches should adopt a flexible coaching style to manage both the situation and personalities involved. They should also help performers to modify their attributions so they have greater control over their actions. This can help motivate performers to improve.

Coaches can help performers take greater responsibility by helping them to reduce their reliance upon external attributions which are typical after poor performances and rephrase them as internal attributions. For example, a tennis player might say 'I was lucky to get away with that one when the ball hits the net and falls in' (ie external attribution/luck). A knowledgeable coach with good communication skills can help the performer change the attribution to 'I accept if I work at lifting the ball a little more, I can ensure it will clear the net cleanly' (ie internal attribution/ability). The performer has changed from a situation where he felt no control to one where he has greater control. The performer who accepts responsibility for the outcome will be motivated to improve the stroke so the skill can be executed better next time.

1.8 Motivating Groups

The motivation of groups, teams or squads is more complex – not only is it a function of the individual and the situation (see Page 2) but it is complicated by the inter-relationships between members of the group and between the group and leader (ie the coach, captain, team manager). Therefore, coaches need to understand about group dynamics – how groups form, develop and interact.

Group Development

Group behaviour constantly changes – groups are either in the early stages of formation, unsettled by the arrival or departure of individuals, struggling to develop group norms, or reacting to success or failure. The following panel describes the typical stages through which groups tend to go.

Researchers suggest that most groups or teams go through these stages at various times:

- **Forming** is where individuals first come together (eg teams, representative squads). Relationships develop between the coach/manager/captain and group members, and the group identifies their goal. Coaches can assist in this process through activities such as ensuring the team warms up, socialises and trains together.

- **Storming** often happens when internal conflicts develop and resistance to any form of control results in rebellion against the coach/manager/captain. Holding open discussions may help to raise issues to enable the group to resolve any conflicts.

- **Norming** is where stability and group cohesion develop as the resistance is overcome; members cooperate as they accept specific roles.

- **Performing** is where group members resolve issues regarding the structure of the group, relations between members stabilise and the group direct their energies towards achieving the goal.

The duration of each stage varies depending on the group. They will fluctuate between these stages especially when the composition changes and new members strive to establish themselves and seek acceptance.

actionplus

Many groups (eg representative teams) encounter problems because of a regular turnover of performers (eg retirement, promotion, transfer, injury and lack of motivation). New performers require time to adjust to the team, establish a rapport with existing members and learn new routines. The challenge for coaches is to integrate new performers into an established group. This process of integration is part of the group's lifecycle (see Figure 6) which comprises four phases:

- **Inclusion** is where performers new to the group try to establish where they fit in, whether they will be liked and whether or not they are good enough.

- **Assertion** is where performers build relationships, establish positions, identify objectives, resolve conflict and form sub-groups.

- **Independence** is where performers accept responsibilities, there is a settled strategy, mutual respect and often complacency.

- **Exclusion** is where performers face the ordeal of being dropped or dealing with failure.

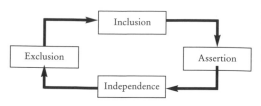

Figure 6: The group lifecycle

Research suggests that groups with a high rate of turnover or short life-cycle are less successful than more stable ones. Therefore, it is important that groups consist of more performers than are necessary to compete at any one time (ie squads). This extends the group's lifecycle and gives new members time to establish themselves and to know the other members of the team before being called on to perform. In this way the group develops cohesion (see next section) and maintains a degree of stability which enables the members to produce consistent performances.

Group Cohesion

Developing squads gives performers the opportunity to bond together (referred to as cohesion). This is the support provided by a group for all its members. It occurs when a group of performers unite in pursuit of a goal and the whole group becomes greater than the sum of its parts. Generally motivation in cohesive groups is high. A group that is not reaching its potential usually has a problem in the way the members interact, make decisions and/or support each other (ie its cohesive structure). Cohesive groups work together to reach and sometimes surpass their potential (eg Liverpool Football Club in the 1980s). Research shows that cohesive teams have:

- more success in competition
- less absenteeism from training sessions
- fewer dropouts
- less conflict
- better communication
- greater commitment to achieving the group goals.

Cohesion plays an essential role in team sports; it brings performers together in the pursuit of a common goal. A cohesive group has many valuable qualities that typically include:

- good teamwork
- strong team spirit
- acceptable and clear goals
- mutual respect and trust
- a willingness to make sacrifices for fellow team members
- high motivation.

Performers in cohesive groups feel more secure, less anxious, more open to change, and willing to accept personal responsibility for group results. Coaches should encourage groups and teams to strive to become cohesive units. Several factors can help improve cohesion in a group (eg similarity of background and shared attitudes, beliefs, motives). Some of these are beyond the coaches' direct control. However, coaches can influence the group:

- size
- communication
- experiences.

Group Size

Performers can potentially remain uninvolved for long periods in large group practices[1]. Each sport will differ but finding the ideal group size for coaching encourages all performers to involve themselves so the group values, and benefits from, their contribution. For example, a hockey coach could have forwards, midfield players and defenders working in separate groups before bringing them together to work on the team's strategy.

---

1   This is referred to as **social loafing** in psychology texts.

Group Communication

Fostering an environment that emphasises a sense of belonging where performers can express opinions, concerns and grievances without fear of ridicule or punishment can help to develop cohesion.

The following techniques help to build group cohesion and enhance motivation:

- encourage frank exchanges of opinion in structured discussion sessions
- promote group identity (eg team kit, clothing, songs)
- highlight the group's traditions and achievements
- develop group pride (eg standards of behaviour and dress)
- encourage the use of the terms **we** and **us.**

Group Experiences

Individuals in sports groups interact in a variety of ways that can either hinder or enhance group cohesion and motivation but coaches can enhance this in the following ways:

- place group members in close proximity but away from other groups prior to performance (eg group huddles on the field of play or bring the team together in the changing room)
- organise enjoyable group social activities to provide non-competitive opportunities for interaction
- increase perceptions of a threat to the group from an outside source – this encourages the group to work together to overcome the threat
- promote group satisfaction by increasing competitive success over an extended period through careful goal setting.

TASK

Consider the problems of selecting a team for competition. Should the selectors choose the individual with high motivation who attends every practice but who is an average performer? Should they choose the performer with the natural talent who shows little interest in the team but always performs well in competition? Consider the effect on team motivation in both cases. How would you deal with this in your sport?

Group Goals

Usually the group has a predetermined goal or purpose for its existence (eg to win the league, to provide an opportunity for people to compete in sport, to act as a social centre). Group members also have their own objectives (eg to perform at the highest level, to improve their proficiency, to gain social approval). The challenge for the coach, manager or captain is to establish and achieve the group's goal, and simultaneously help individuals within the group to achieve their personal goal.

Through open discussions, each performer has an opportunity to air their views and decide the group goal. An agreed, clear and achievable goal (see Section 1.3, Page 5) helps to focus the group, raise individual and group motivation, and develop group cohesion. The group then takes on the ownership of the goal because each member has been involved in deciding and shaping it.

Each member of the group also takes on a degree of responsibility for achieving the goal. This collective ownership and responsibility helps the goal become more intrinsically motivating for performers. It also helps to create a no-blame culture where everyone takes responsibility for the group's success and failure (see Page 22).

An effective coach, manager or captain will discuss the best way for each of their performers to achieve their personal goals. This enables the group and individuals within the group to achieve their goals simultaneously. In this way the goals complement rather than conflict with each other.

1.9 Group Leadership

The skill of the leader is a significant factor in developing highly motivated groups. A good coach, captain or manager can help stimulate and motivate performers to improve themselves and to help the group achieve its peak potential. Three factors affect the leadership style and group cohesion:

- **Leader behaviour** – where leaders are responsible for encouraging performers to work together towards achieving the group goal. This involves establishing and developing strategies to attain the group goal

- **Decision-making style** – where the use of a democratic decision style encourages cohesion and develops individual motivation by involving performers. These performers are more likely to share credit for successes and accept responsibility when things go wrong. The most effective way to decide is to have all performers present and involve them in the discussions.

- **Leader-performer compatibility –** where the effectiveness of the working relationship between the leader and performer is important to group cohesion. It does not necessarily mean the two agree on every issue; very different members of a group can be compatible. It is important that the leader and performers resolve their differences, work together and complement each other.

TASK

If you are a leader (eg coach, captain), think about your leadership style. If you are a performer, think about the leaders with whom you have worked.

How successful was the style of leadership in developing a cohesive and effective group or team?

Did the performers respond positively to the style?

What could be done to improve the leadership style?

To help compatibility, coaches, managers or captains should aim to:

- clarify a series of democratically agreed goals
- clarify the individual roles of group members
- provide feedback about individual performances
- use rewards appropriately and fairly
- be open-minded and flexible (eg adapting coaching sessions, seeking advice, encouraging feedback from performers)

- develop mutual respect and trust (eg delegating responsibility, listening and responding to feedback from performers)
- listen to and encourage contributions from performers (eg providing opportunities for open discussion)
- understand and appreciate their diverse roles and responsibilities (eg an instructor, teacher, friend, guardian)
- know their performers (eg friends, family, motives, interests).

Group Rewards

Performers can receive rewards from a variety of sources (eg the coach, other performers, themselves). Appropriate rewards given to individual performers can enhance motivation (see Section 1.4, Page 8). However, rewards can both help and hinder group cohesiveness. Coaches, managers and/or captains should decide in advance whether rewards are for:

- the most successful performers
- those who show the most progress
- those who try the hardest
- all performers.

sports coach UK

Problems can occur in a group when not everyone receives a reward – some individuals may feel their contribution or involvement is not valued. This may prevent the group from reaching its full potential. Leaders should ensure they value each of their performers and their contribution to the group.

TASK

The Yellow Jersey Strategy for motivating young performers illustrates one motivational strategy currently in use with a group of young performers:

Goals: Performers demonstrate physical effort in training, a positive, cooperative attitude towards technical problems, self-discipline, improving ability.

Reward: The performer wears the yellow jersey in training for one week.

Rules: Four coaching staff judge who wears the yellow jersey and they present it every Wednesday before the training session.

Think of a strategy you can use to enhance motivation of performers in your sport.

Taking responsibility

The way group members perceive different situations can influence group cohesion. Motivation will rise or fall following competition depending on whether or not the group achieves success. For example, a performer who attributes a poor performance to personal factors (eg lack of ability) is likely to lose motivation. In team sports the performer and coach, manager and/or captain can view the same outcome from a slightly different perspective based on their personal experiences. For example, following a goal, defenders blame the goalkeeper for poor positioning, the goalkeeper blames the defenders for not marking the opposing forwards, and the coach blames the midfield players for losing possession in the first place. Coaches and performers should try to develop a **no-blame culture** where everyone takes collective responsibility for success and failure.

Midway through a finely balanced rugby international (Wales v England 1993), Rory Underwood – one of the world's finest wingers – had a momentary lapse of concentration. This allowed his opponent to score a try. The match ended in a 10–9 win for Wales.

At the post match press conference, the English media were calling for Underwood's head, attributing the blame for England's defeat on his one mistake. Geoff Cooke, the England manager at the time, defended his player by reminding the press that one mistake did not suddenly make Underwood a poor player. Cooke reminded the press of all the wonderful (possibly match winning) tries that Underwood had scored in the past for England. He questioned how the press could attribute Underwood's single error as the cause of the defeat when there were many other errors during the game (eg missed scoring chances, technical errors). No questions were asked of the player who conceded a penalty kick which allowed Wales to score three more points.

By creating a no-blame culture, Cooke successfully managed to alter the media's perception so the team took collective responsibility for defeat. All groups or teams should strive to develop this cohesive and supportive culture where everyone accepts responsibility for success or failure.

Objective analysis of performance (eg match analysis, statistical data, performance times, judging scores) is important to ensure the feedback is free from bias (ie either from the coach or performers or both), clear for all to see and adds positively to group cohesion. When linked with a no-blame culture, objective analysis should help to foster group cohesion and motivation.

1.10 Summary

To help performers increase and maintain their motivation, coaches need to establish each performer's personal motives. Next they need to use these motives to design stimulating and challenging practices and sessions that help motivate performers to improve. Performers will only want to improve their performance if they feel comfortable in the coaching environment. They can then try new and different approaches, ask questions and discover for themselves without the fear of being ridiculed or put down. Coaches set the tone of the environment through the way they communicate with the performers (ie give praise, positive and corrective feedback, encourage questions). The success of coaching environments in helping performers to improve and form cohesive groups depends on the coach's relationship with each performer. Therefore coaches should talk regularly to each performer and try to establish a good working relationship. Knowing each performer well enables the coach to offer appropriate support, advice and guidance when the performer needs it in competition.

Recommended Reading

Other books providing information on motivation:

Carron, A.V. (1984) *Motivation Implications for Coaching and Teaching.* London, Ontario: Sports Dynamics. ISBN: 0-969161-90-5. (*out of print*)

Cox, R. (2002) *Sport Psychology: Concepts and Applications.* London: McGraw-Hill. ISBN: 0-072329-14-9.

Kerr, J.H. (1999) *Motivation and Emotion in Sport: Reversal Theory.* Hove: Psychology Press. ISBN: 0-863775-00-4.

Roberts, G. (2001) *Advances in Motivation in Sport and Exercise.* Champaign, IL: Human Kinetics. ISBN: 0-880118-49-0.

You are also recommended to the following **scUK** workshops and resources (see Pages 68–70 for further details):

– *Coaching Disabled Performers*
– *Coaching Methods and Communication*
– *Coaching Young Performers*
– *Goal-setting and Planning*
– *Improving Practices and Skill*
– *Performance Profiling*

TASK

The list of qualities of a highly motivated performer from the first task in this chapter (Page 3) should enable you to have a good picture of a highly motivated performer. The answers to the questions from the task on Page 19 should enable you to determine what your performers require to be highly motivated individuals. Combining these pieces of information with the remaining information in this chapter, you can probably suggest two changes you can make to the following:

• the structure of one practice in your next coaching session

• the structure of your next coaching session

• the coaching environment

• your coaching behaviour.

This may not be an easy task to complete. However, if you successfully manage to make the changes, you will have made significant changes to your coaching practice. This will be directly helping to motivate and improve your performers. You should repeat this exercise periodically to improve the quality of your coaching and enhance each performer's development.

CHAPTER TWO:
Developing Mental Toughness

2.0 Introduction

Why do performers have good days and bad days? Why does their performance fluctuate?

Successful performance often involves more than simply superior skills and physical preparation – it seems that mental factors frequently distinguish the winner from the loser, the consistent from the erratic performer, the outstanding from the average performance. In addition to honing technical/tactical proficiency and physical condition, coaches also need to ensure their performers are mentally tough. They need to help them develop a number of mental qualities (the four Cs[1]):

- **Commitment** to strive for their goals
- **Confidence** (self-confidence) in their ability to succeed
- **Control** (emotional control) to focus their energy on the goal
- **Concentration** to achieve their goals.

Some performers – usually the elite – regularly exhibit many of these qualities. However, the majority struggle to display these components of mental toughness. The challenge for coaches is to help performers develop these qualities to a level where they are able to maximise training sessions and achieve peak performances consistently in competition. This can be achieved by modifying how goals are set and adjusted, how coaching practices and sessions are structured, and how preparations are made for competitions.

Mental skills are techniques used by performers to help them attain these qualities. They have been shown to help performers focus attention and avoid distraction, enhance and maintain self-confidence and control anxiety. Mental skills are as important in everyday life as they are in sport and can be learned and developed through appropriate practice in the same way sports skills are acquired.

1   The development of these four mental qualities is the main focus of the **scUK** home study pack *Mental Skills: An Introduction for Sports Coaches*, available from Coachwise 1st4sport on 0113-201 5555 or via www.1st4sport.com

2.1 Increasing Commitment

Anyone striving to attain their goals and improve their performance, needs commitment. Committed performers tend to work on all aspects of their sport – techniques, tactics, physical condition, mental skills – with minimum supervision because they understand what they are trying to achieve and possess the desire to achieve it. The achievement of long-term aims may require dedication over a number of years. However, with commitment, performers can make steady progress. There are three stages in establishing and maintaining commitment:

- determining the performer's aims and ambitions
- identifying any conflicting interests
- converting aims into goals.

Determining Aims and Ambitions

Most performers have dreams or aims about what they want to achieve in their sport and successful coaches[1] use these as the basis on which to develop their programmes. Therefore, the coach's first task is to help performers identify their aims and ambitions.

Coaches must invest time with each performer to develop a good working relationship and build up a picture of each one's long-term ambition and potential, and current strengths and weaknesses. The act of sharing a personal aim or ambition can be a sensitive issue for some performers, so coaches need to:

- select an appropriate time for the discussion
- be supportive and reassuring
- encourage openness and honesty by reassuring them that all discussions are confidential
- demonstrate good communication skills (ie tact, diplomacy, sensitivity).

---

1 For further information about the coach's role refer to the **scUK** resource *The Successful Coach*, available from Coachwise 1st4sport on 0113-201 5555 or via www.1st4sport.com

Identifying Conflicting Interests

Coaches and performers will each have many interests and demands in their lives in addition to their sport (eg family, studying, school, work, hobbies and friends). Therefore, before agreeing and committing to any training programme, performers and coaches should establish what other factors compete for time and attention. Once these are established, it is easier to determine the amount of time and energy they can commit to the development of their sporting talent. It is important to go through this process so the coach and performer are aware of each other's level of commitment, are realistic about what they can achieve together and share the same expectations.

Converting Aims into Goals

Aims and ambitions refer to what performers would like to achieve. To turn these into a reality requires the careful setting of goals – long-term, intermediate and short-term goals – and then the structuring of an appropriate plan to achieve them. Short-term and intermediate goals enable performers to achieve success on a regular basis while still working towards the long-term goal. Success encourages performers to maintain their commitment as well as build their self-confidence. Therefore, effective goal setting is vital to both commitment and self-confidence (the process of goal setting was discussed in more detail in Section 1.3, Page 5).

sports coach UK

SUMMARY

Coaches can help performers develop commitment by:

- working together to identify their aims and ambitions

- identifying any interests which may conflict with the performer's training

- converting aims and ambitions into long-term, intermediate and short-term SMART goals.

2.2 Self-confidence

Performers with high self-confidence believe they can carry out an action successfully; performers with low self-confidence perceive they cannot. Self-confidence helps people to feel good about themselves, encourages them to try new techniques and overcome difficult challenges.

Therefore, it is a really important factor in sport (eg in tennis it has been shown to be one of the factors which differentiates highly from less successful players[1]). Coaches need to create practices, sessions and environments which provide performers with the opportunity to feel competent and develop their self-confidence.

Coaches need to create a *performance highway* (see Figure 7, Page 40) for their performers – recognising that the more success performers experience in sport situations, the greater their self-confidence becomes in those situations.

Self-confidence can be enhanced in four main ways[2]:

- through goal achievement (setting and achieving SMART goals)

- through vicarious experience (ie watching other performers carry out a skill successfully)

- with verbal persuasion (ie self-talk 'I can do it'; coach reinforcement 'you can do it')

- by the appropriate interpretation of physiological cues (ie increased heart rate, rapid breathing).

Goal Achievement

Effective goal setting helps performers to achieve goals and improve their self-confidence, which in turn helps to focus attention on key issues (concentration), reduce anxiety and improve skills.

The level at which a goal is set can increase or decrease a performer's level of anxiety – a factor that all too often undermines confidence.

1   Weinberg, R.S. (1988) *The Mental Advantage: Developing Your Psychological Skills in Tennis.* Champaign, IL: Human Kinetics. ISBN: 0-880112-93-X.

2   Feelings of competence and confidence in a sports situation have been explained by Bandura's theory of self-efficacy. Bandura, A. (1977) *Social Learning Theory.* Englewood Cliffs NJ: Prentice Hall. ISBN: 0-148167-51-6.

Most performers set themselves goals that are too hard rather than too easy; a goal which was acceptable during training can become unacceptable to a performer under the stress of competition. This can increase a performer's level of anxiety. The research suggests that anxiety can reduce a performer's acceptance of a goal by as much as 40%. If performers do not accept a goal they are less likely to achieve it. This can result in a decrease in self-confidence if the performer fails to achieve the desired goal (see Figure 4 on Page 21).

actionplus

Performers who set goals beyond their ability may show short-term improvements in performance. However, in the long-term, consistent failure to achieve the goals will lead to self-criticism and a decrease in self-confidence.

If a performer sets a training goal of ten straight arm pull-ups and actually completes ten, the goal has been achieved. The goal may then be reset to 12 pull-ups, which is subsequently achieved.

If the goal had been reset to 14, the achievement of 12 pull-ups would have been deemed a failure by the performer (albeit a performance improvement, even a personal best) with the resultant loss in confidence in ability.

A good coach should help the performer to understand why the goal was unsuccessful (ie too little time for physiological adaptation) and help him to set a more realistic goal (ie three sets of 14 repetitions) which maintains the performer's confidence or self-efficacy.

Coaches and performers should adjust goals before competitive events to ensure self-confidence is raised (or at least maintained), performance is optimised and success is achieved.

To build confidence, it may help to think of the ABC of goal setting. Goals need to be:

- **achievable** – clear, specific and measurable – performers need to know they have achieved them

- **believable** – goals must be realistic, accepted by the performers and yet challenging – this may best be achieved by providing a step by step progression – stepping stones to success

- **controllable** – goals need to be under the control of the performer (ie the performer can control the run time, distance jumped, percentage shots played; it is not possible to control winning and losing).

Goals should also be reviewed and adjusted regularly – self-confidence is often fragile and in a constant state of change.

The challenge for coaches is to ensure performers stay in the success lane of the performance highway (see Figure 7). If performers perceive the challenge to be too low, they will be bored and under-perform (comfort or boredom lanes). If performers perceive the challenge to exceed their ability, they will become anxious (enter the anxiety lane) and under-perform[1].

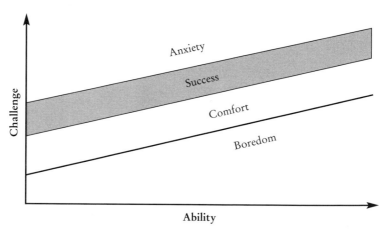

Figure 7: The performance highway

1   This concept is considered again in relation to anxiety on Page 49.

Vicarious Experience

Observing others being successful can inspire performers to develop skills and achieve goals. Through observation, performers can generate images to help them copy a new technique, which in turn can increase proficiency and confidence. Performers may gain from observing famous international performers, other club performers or the coach.

However, vicarious experience must be realistic if it is to be of value – there is little point in a 2.5m basketball player demonstrating a dunk shot to a group of 1.6m players who cannot possibly perform the skill in the same way. Coaches can show video recordings of performers with a high level of skill carrying out an action or they can mix skilled and less skilled performers in groups to encourage the less skilled to learn from the more skilled performers.

TASK

Coaches rarely capitalise fully on the potential impact of vicarious experience as a means of developing skill and building confidence. How often do you plan coaching sessions to ensure that less skilled performers are able to observe more experienced performers practising?

Verbal Persuasion

This refers to both exhortations by the coach (eg 'you can do it') as well as positive self-talk by the performer (eg 'I can do it'). Self-talk is a form of verbal persuasion which can significantly improve self-confidence and performance by replacing the all-too-familiar negative thoughts (eg 'I give up, I can't do it') and doubts.

Self-talk can focus on:

- **technique** where words or phrases are used as cues to trigger actions (ie punch in a tennis volley; spot the wall, plant and drive in executing a tumble turn in swimming)

- **effect** where verbal cues are used to enhance performance (ie power to emphasise the release in javelin throwing, 'b' of the bang in a sprint start)

- **affirmation** where regular positive statements are given to enhance self-confidence (ie 'I trained well today; I feel strong, fit and confident in my own ability').

TASK

Think of one situation recently where you have used negative self talk in your sport.

To what aspect of the performance did the comment actually relate?

What factor(s) triggered the negative self talk?

Next time, how will you recognise when you are about to speak negatively to yourself?

How can you use positive self talk to change this situation?

Coaches should help performers to recognise the situations when the performers use negative self-talk and encourage them to change these to positive statements (see following panel). They should also allow performers to experiment with and establish their own positive verbal cues which relate to specific techniques and have a special meaning to each performer.

There are also a number of mental skills (eg imagery[1]) that performers can use to help them remain confident in spite of the demands and challenges of the situation.

actionplus

1   This is considered in more detail in Section 2.5 on Page 56.

Negative	Positive
These conditions don't suit me. ⟶	Nobody likes this weather; I can play as well as anyone in these conditions.
I can't lose. ⟶	If I stick to the game plan and give my best, I'll be OK.
I'll never keep this up for three more sets. ⟶	That was hard but I did it; I'll really go for the last three.

Interpreting Physiological Cues

Increased heart rate, butterflies in the stomach and shortage of breath are all natural body responses to some form of a challenge – a threat, an exam, a sports competition. The way the mind interprets these physiological sensations can influence self-confidence. For example, prior to competition it can be construed negatively as anxiety[1] or positively as a feeling of readiness or preparation for action. Coaches can encourage performers to remain confident by helping them interpret these physiological cues positively.

SUMMARY

Self-confidence can help performers to attempt new challenges, recover quickly from disappointment, enjoy their sports involvement and above all perform to their potential.

It is vital that coaches and performers work on ways to build and maintain high levels of confidence through effective goal setting, the judicious use of vicarious experience and verbal persuasion, as well as the accurate interpretation of physiological cues.

1   This is considered in more detail in Section 2.4 on Page 48.

2.3 Concentration

The ability to gain and maintain concentration during a sports event is frequently deemed to be crucial to ultimate success. Studies show expert sports performers are able to pay attention to relevant information or cues, anticipate the outcome and make appropriate responses better than novices. Performers with good concentration skills are able to focus on the here and now. They are not readily distracted by past events (eg a mistake, an unfavourable decision) nor by possible outcomes (eg 'what if I lose? If I win the next game, I'll be the champion'). Their attention is focused on what is currently happening.

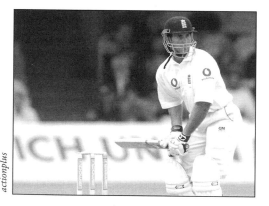

actionplus

Where should attention be focused? This will depend on the sport, the specific situation and even the level of skill of the performer. Performers

should be able to adapt their focus of attention to these relevant cues. For example, a cricket batsman may watch the position of the fielders prior to the delivery but should then switch attention to the run-up and arm of the bowler, and then to the ball itself. All these are examples of external cues – the fielders, the bowler, the ball. There may also be times when the batsmen should turn their attention internally – to draw on previous experience of the bowler's strengths, to rehearse a forward defensive drive or to review a stroke just executed to determine why it was mistimed.

Attentional Styles

Attention needs to be placed in different places at different times. Individuals also seem to exhibit certain preferences or attentional styles. The continuum of **width** refers to whether attention is narrowly focused (eg on the ball, on a particular joint action) or more broadly focused (eg onto the whole court, to a range of tactical possibilities). Attentional **direction** refers to an internal focus (eg to the performer's own thoughts and feelings) or externally (to the events happening outside the body). Figure 8 provides examples of each type of attentional style.

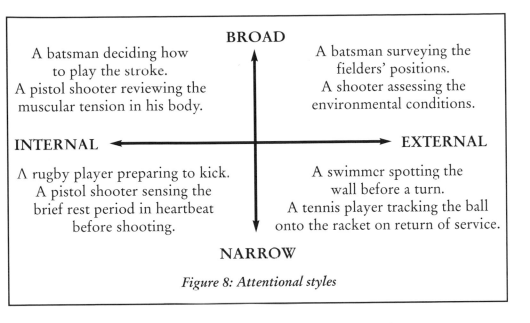

BROAD

A batsman deciding how to play the stroke.
A pistol shooter reviewing the muscular tension in his body.

A batsman surveying the fielders' positions.
A shooter assessing the environmental conditions.

INTERNAL ⟵————————⟶ **EXTERNAL**

A rugby player preparing to kick.
A pistol shooter sensing the brief rest period in heartbeat before shooting.

A swimmer spotting the wall before a turn.
A tennis player tracking the ball onto the racket on return of service.

NARROW

Figure 8: Attentional styles

Therefore, there is a time to turn attention inward to analyse what is happening, plan strategy and monitor bodily responses, and there is a time to turn attention externally to examine the environmental conditions, the opposition and the goal, target or outcome of an action. Basketball players may have to alter their focus throughout a game – a broad internal focus when assessing the opposition before making a pass; a narrow external focus when taking a free throw.

Distractions can also be internal (eg negative thoughts, pain from an injury) or external (eg audience, officials, opposition, playing conditions).

Both can affect a performer's attention and concentration. They can occur for all sorts of reasons – for example disinterest, worry, discomfort and unfamiliarity (eg sound of the crowd, loud music, aircraft, floodlights).

An individual's level of anxiety can affect concentration which can prove critical. Neil Adams (British Judo Champion) competing for the gold medal in the Seoul Olympics 1988 was momentarily distracted by a call from the opposition's coach. Neil's concentration (focus of attention) became temporarily disrupted which cost him the winning throw.

Improving Concentration

Coaches can help performers to improve concentration in a number of ways. For example, trigger words (eg watch the spin, keep it smooth) can be used to focus attention in the same way they can be used to increase confidence and raise motivation. These, combined with the development of set routines, can be especially useful to focus attention and reduce anxiety on set pieces (eg at the free throw line in basketball, prior to the vault in gymnastics). In addition, certain mental skills can be used to suppress distractions (eg black box technique[1]), or help focus attention on key issues and positive images (eg imagery[2]). Coaching practices can also be devised to improve concentration and eliminate distractions (example in panel).

Distraction games have also been used successfully. Performers from one group practise sports skills while another group deliberately tries to distract them without using physical force. The performers practising their sports skills learn how to maintain

Inner Tennis, a learning strategy devised by Tim Gallwey[3], used a number of practices to avoid negative self-talk and anxiety, and focus on the ball and feeling of the movement. These drills included:

- calling out aloud *bounce* and *hit* as the ball struck the ground and then the racket
- watching the seams of the ball and calling out the direction of ball spin (back, side or top)
- estimating the height of the oncoming ball over the net to focus attention on ball flight.

their focus of attention while being distracted. Sessions must be structured to ensure they are safe and include a variety of distractions to help performers to develop their concentration skills (eg poor refereeing decisions, crowds, verbal criticism, intimidating opposition).

Performers can use cues to trigger and focus their concentration. They can also develop object focusing

1   This involves placing a distracting or worrying thought in an imaginary black box during a particular event (eg competition) and then investing time in addressing the concern after the event.

2   This is considered in more detail in Section 2.5 on Page 56.

3   Gallwey, W.T. (1986) *The inner game of tennis.* London: Pan Books. ISBN: 0-330295-13-6.

techniques to help them concentrate on one specific task at a time (eg visual cue – looking at the strings on the tennis racket; verbal cues – strong, power, control; kinaesthetic cue – the feel of a successfully executed gymnastic skill).

Coaches should encourage performers to practise each of the four types of attention focus (broad, narrow, internal, external) while they are going through distraction training so they become proficient in changing their focus of attention successfully in competitive situations as the demands of the sport require. Coaches can structure simulated competitive situations and introduce the competitive variables in a controlled way so performers can gradually learn the strategies to cope with the demands of competition.

Coaches need to help performers identify and concentrate on significant cues and eliminate distractions. Coaches who know the main factors which distract attention can help performers to recognise distractions and devise strategies to counter them. This can be achieved through the careful selection of drills and practices, the identification of appropriate attentional focus in a range of situations and the simulation of distracting situations.

TASK

Consider the problem of a basketball player who constantly criticises and is easily distracted by refereeing decisions. The player's concentration will not be appropriately focused (eg the player may be focused on her anger with the other players/referee or her frustration with the score line) and several mistakes may occur (eg unnecessary fouls, missed shots and poor positional play).

To help this player develop appropriate concentration skills, she first needs to learn strategies (eg trigger words) to help refocus attention. Once this technique has been mastered, the coach can simulate unfavourable refereeing decisions in training sessions. The player must use the triggers to focus attention. The number of bad decisions can be increased and eventually used in practice without warning.

Are there performers that you coach who require help with concentration? How would you structure sessions to help them?

2.4 Emotional Control

Performers experience a wide range of emotions when competing in sport (ie joy, frustration, anger, satisfaction). These emotions, although part of normal behaviour, can become potential sources of distraction and interference if they are not managed appropriately. While performers are experiencing these emotions, their concentration will not be focused on the task and the probability of success is greatly reduced. The task is unlikely to be executed efficiently, effectively or performed at all. Therefore, it is important that coaches help performers learn how to control their emotions so they can channel their energy and focus their attention on successfully achieving the task. The most commonly experienced and disruptive emotions are probably stress and anxiety – they have a significant effect on sports performance.

Stress and Anxiety

Numerous terms are used to describe stress and anxiety – eg panic, nerves, worry, activation and arousal. The rest of this section looks at these emotions in further detail and explains their effect on performance.

Stress is a psychological concept which can be positive or negative. It is based on a performer's perception of their ability in relation to the demands of the situation. It can affect the performer's ability to attend to relevant cues, make decisions and execute actions. The performer's reaction to the perception of stress is the most critical factor for sports performance. If a situation is perceived positively, performers interpret the events as challenging, exciting and exhilarating. If a situation is perceived negatively, the situation is seen as threatening and performers worry about their ability to cope. Studies show performers who perceive stress to be positive:

- are high in self-confidence
- have a clear picture of what is required
- maintain focused concentration.

Performers who perceive stress to be negative on the other hand:

- are low in self-confidence
- uncertain about the outcome (often characterised by a fear of failure)
- have difficulty concentrating.

If the latter situation remains unchanged, performers will experience increasing levels of negative stress and anxiety.

Anxiety describes the negative reactions to stress which can disrupt performance by generating worry and impairing the way performers process information. Feelings of threat are often experienced and are typically brought about by different situations such as:

- fear of physical harm (eg being tackled in rugby, hit by the ball or stick in hockey)
- threat to the ego or self-image (ie being beaten by a lower ranked player)
- fear of punishment (eg fines, post match debrief after a loss, retribution by a coach or manager, being dropped).

Some individuals appear to have a greater general susceptibility to anxiety than others – this is part of their personality make-up and is referred to as **trait anxiety.** Irrespective of personality factors, most performers experience the unpleasant tension in certain situations (eg before the start of a competition). This is referred to as **state anxiety.** It is helpful for coaches to differentiate these types of anxiety and for both coaches and performers to recognise the symptoms of anxiety. These are often grouped into two categories:

- **Cognitive symptoms** are the psychological responses to thoughts about the forthcoming performance (ie worry[1], negative thinking, poor concentration, insomnia). They are related to expectations about the performance and often increase 24–48 hours (or even a week) prior to competition.

- **Somatic symptoms** are the physiological responses (arousal[2]) to thoughts about the forthcoming performance (ie rapid pulse rate, sweating, increased muscle tension). They usually occur nearer to the event than cognitive symptoms (approximately 60–90 minutes before) and are directly related to information associated with performance (ie arriving at the event, hearing the crowd, seeing the opposition for the first time).

---

1   The term **worry** is therefore used to describe the unpleasant thoughts which accompany anxiety (eg fear of failure).

2   **Arousal** is usually used to refer to the physiological responses which accompany anxiety and stress.

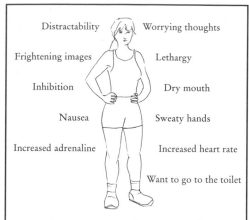

Figure 9: Symptoms of worry and arousal

Distractability
Worrying thoughts
Frightening images
Lethargy
Inhibition
Dry mouth
Nausea
Sweaty hands
Increased adrenaline
Increased heart rate
Want to go to the toilet

Coaches need to be able to recognise these symptoms (see Figure 9) as well as the potential positive and negative effects on performance. Typical negative effects can impact on every stage – perception (interpretation of information), decision making and execution:

- attention – whether or not cues are picked up (eg poor concentration, panic)

- decision making (eg indecision, reverting to tried and trusted techniques, limited imagination, over cautious)

- the way the movement is executed (eg trying too hard, increased muscle tension will interfere with the smooth well organised movement pattern).

However, a certain level of arousal or anxiety also appears to have a positive effect. Why?

Effect of Anxiety on Performance

Stress and anxiety have a direct impact on sports performance depending on how they are perceived by performers. The relationship between anxiety and performance is often explained by the **Inverted-U hypothesis.** This states that increases in performance correspond with increases in stress to a certain point after which further increases in stress result in decreased performance (see Figure 10).

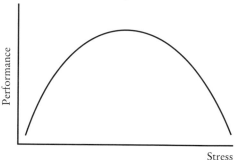

Figure 10: The stress-performance relationship predicted for experienced performers using the Inverted-U hypothesis

This implies that to regain optimal performance, all that is required is a reduction in stress levels. However, experience shows that performers who are over-stressed have to reduce their stress levels consciously to regain any level of performance.

Although stress can lead to increased physiological arousal (eg increased heart rate, sweaty hands, butterflies), some highly anxious performers may not exhibit these signs. The Inverted-U hypothesis is therefore generally regarded as an over-simplification of the effects of stress on performance.

More recently, an alternative explanation has been proposed – the **Catastrophe hypothesis** (Figure 11). This suggests that at low stress levels, performance improves up to a critical threshold. At this point performers start to perceive an imbalance between the demands of the situation and their ability to cope (ie they experience negative stress). This results in a sudden increase in anxiety and performance dramatically drops.

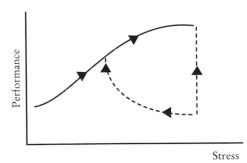

Figure 11: The stress-performance relationship for experienced performers using the Catastrophe hypothesis

The original level of performance can only be regained if stress levels are reduced to the point where the two curves are closest which allows performers to return to the upper curve (eg temporarily substituting players in basketball or hockey and allowing them time to lower their stress levels before they return to the game; in more extreme cases performers dropping down into lower teams and competitions while they establish emotional control).

To avoid the negative effects of stress and anxiety, performers need to learn emotional control techniques (Section 2.5, Page 56) and coaches need to be able to reduce the perceived demand on the performer, improve the performer's ability or both.

To gain the greatest benefits of positive stress and arousal, coaches need to help performers learn to raise the arousal levels to the optimal level – push them to the edge of the cliff but not over. Coaches therefore need to devise ways to help performers reduce the negative aspects of anxiety and optimise their mental and physical state prior to performance.

However the impact of anxiety on performance seems to be complicated by three factors:

- the individual (ie personality factors, experience)
- the type of sport/skill
- the level/perception of the demand.

Individual Differences

Individual physical and emotional (psychological) differences arise as a result of a combination of genetic factors and environmental experiences. The differences affect the way performers respond to stress and anxiety and can influence the way they cope with both successful and unsuccessful performances (see Figure 12). The Type A[1] individual tends to thrive on higher levels of stress – they seek greater challenges and pressure, and often make rapid improvements in performance in this climate. Their success lane on the performance highway (see Figure 7, Page 40) is higher and steeper – the level at which stress provokes anxiety is higher and they are able to achieving higher levels of

performance more quickly than the Type B person (Figure 12a and 12b). However, if the stress forces the performance into the anxiety lane, the fall off in performance is more dramatic – they fall further down the cliff – the resulting performance loss is greater and it takes much longer to restore confidence and regain the previous performance levels (Fig 13).

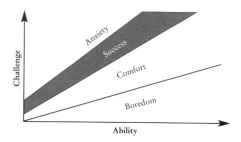

Fig 12a: Performance highways for Type A individuals (Fearless Vera)

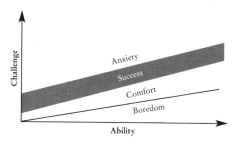

Fig 12b: Performance highways for Type B individuals (Steady Eddie)

---

1   Type A and B individuals describe personality types – Type A is used to describe someone who likes to live life in the fast lane, enjoys challenges and stress, typically extrovert – the Fearless Vera type; Type B prefers to operate in response to more gradual challenges – more the Steady Eddie type.

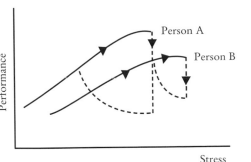

Fig 13: Stress-performance curves for Type A and Type B people

Coaches need to adapt their approach and coaching style to the unique personality type of the individual – help them to stay in the success lane and not veer into the anxiety lane or fall into the comfort zone for both these will result in under-performance.

Coaches must ensure they avoid pushing performers over their personal cliffs.

The success lane for Type B individuals on the other hand is more gradual – they prefer to operate at lower stress levels and may take longer to improve and achieve their potential. However, if they are forced into the anxiety lane because they perceive the demand exceeds their capacity, they typically suffer a smaller decrement in performance (lower cliff) and can more quickly and easily regain their confidence and former performance level (ie return to the success lane). This has considerable implications for coaches – they need to recognise the different personality types, their tolerance of stress and desire for challenge – they need to set goals with performers appropriately and treat each performer differently.

Type of Sport or Skill

When a performer perceives a difficult or threatening situation, the body responds by preparing for action with the flight or fight response. This automatic response has evolved over thousands of generations and prepares the body for an emergency response. Sports performers can trigger this response automatically depending on whether a forthcoming event is perceived as a stressful or threatening situation.

The response can be beneficial for some sports performers – explosive (eg shot put, long jump, karate) or endurance events (eg distance running, cycling, swimming) use a large percentage of the body's muscle mass and so place a great demand on the energy system. In these events the excess energy from increased arousal levels can be channelled into the event with potentially beneficial consequences.

However, sports that rely on fine muscular control and decision making (eg shooting, gymnastics, hockey) are potentially more susceptible to negative effects from the excess energy generated by the flight or fight stress response. Performers in these sports need to develop good emotional control techniques and be offered extensive opportunities to cope with competitive stress.

Level/Perception of Demand

The way that performers perceive the demand (eg the intensity of the training session, the pressure of the competition, the expectations of others) will determine the perception of stress and feelings of anxiety. If they perceive the demand to exceed their ability to succeed, they will experience anxiety which may have a detrimental effect on performance. This perception of demand may explain the varying effects of audiences on performers (see panel).

actionplus

Professional football players often play in front of large, noisy and sometimes abusive crowds. The crowds may be perceived as a source of negative stress to the performers either because of their size, or because of their expectations – each can cause feelings of worry, self doubt and incompetence. Football players need to be able to reduce their anxiety levels, concentrate on their goals and refocus their concentration as necessary to avoid distractions.

Alternatively, the crowd may be perceived as being supportive and encouraging, bolstering self-confidence and encouraging feelings of competence. Whichever way the crowd is perceived, professional football players need the ability to reduce the negative effects of stress and anxiety on performance and enhance the positive aspects of their performance.

SUMMARY

- The extent to which stress and anxiety affect performance varies depending upon the individual, the type of sport/skill, the performer's perception of the demands.

- The challenge to performers and coaches is to maximise the positive effects of stress and anxiety while preventing the negative effects which can disrupt the ability to take in information, make decisions and execute movements skilfully.

Controlling Anxiety

Some performers (and indeed some coaches) assume the only way to learn how to handle anxiety is through repeatedly experiencing it. Therefore, if performers experience anxiety prior to competition, they should be given more actual competition experience. This may be effective but if not, the likelihood is the performer will no longer enjoy competing and will ultimately give up the sport. The assumption also neglects some potentially powerful experiences that can be gained through the careful structuring and management of coaching sessions (training strategies) and through the development of mental skills (eg relaxation skills, use of imagery). These are considered in more detail in the following section.

2.5 Mental Skills

This refers to the way that important mental qualities (eg the four Cs – commitment, confidence, concentration and control) can be strengthened through practice in the same way that physical skills are developed through practice. These skills (eg imagery, relaxation, centring, use of positive statements and routines) can be developed and used in a variety of different situations – in training, prior to, during and following competition, as well as in everyday life. Some are described in the following sections.

Imagery[1]

This is where performers visualise themselves executing a technique well in a forthcoming event or recall themselves performing well in a previous successful event:

- **External imagery** is where performers visualise their own performances as if someone else is watching them (ie similar to looking at a video recording of themselves).

- **Internal imagery** is where performers visualise their actual performance by seeing (ie through their own eyes) and feeling with their own senses (ie intrinsic feedback from the senses, muscles and joints) – experiencing the performance.

There are a number of uses of imagery in sport which include:

- **instant pre-play** – where the performer mentally rehearses a technique immediately prior to carrying it out (ie going through the action in the mind before a tennis serve, a free throw in basketball or golf swing)

- **instant replay** – where the performer imagines a technique immediately after its execution to reinforce the correct movement pattern (ie after the tennis serve, the free throw or the golf swing).

Performers should be encouraged to make use of all their senses while visualising to make the images more vivid – hearing the sound of the bat hitting the ball, seeing the flight of the ball through the air, feeling the precise position of each part of the body in executing the shot.

---

1 For more information on imagery, you are recommended to the **scUK** workshop and resource *Imagery Training* – see Page 69 for further details.

To become proficient in using imagery, performers need to practise the techniques on a regular basis. Coaches should actively encourage performers to use imagery before, during and after physical practice or competition to help improve their technical proficiency in the sport.

actionplus

When used before an event (ie days, hours or instant pre-play), imagery can help to replace negative thoughts, reduce any effects of anxiety and raise confidence.

Immediately prior to a situation (eg at the free throw line in basketball, on the blocks in a sprint event, immediately before a routine in gymnastics), it can also improve concentration and mentally practise the actual execution of the forthcoming action.

After an action, it can provide excellent feedback, be used to identify errors or to reinforce the right movement pattern.

TASK

Considerable practice is required to become proficient in the use of imagery. The following exercise provides an introduction to imagery training techniques:

Preparation: Make yourself comfortable in a chair.

Exercise: Take in a long slow breath, hold for a silent count of three, relax and breathe out slowly. Repeat twice and close your eyes. Think of a pleasant sporting occasion where you performed well. Run the image through your mind at normal speed until you reach the end or until your concentration wavers. Count from one to three and open your eyes.

After the exercise: Did you experience the events as though you were there, seeing, hearing and feeling everything as it happened? This is internal imagery. Did you experience the events as if you were watching a film or video recording of yourself carrying out the action? This is external imagery. Did you switch between the two types?

Relaxation

This describes a range of techniques which can be used to calm the mind and body (ie quieten worry, reduce arousal). Performers can recover their energy levels, thoughts and emotions. Relaxation can reverse the physical and mental effects of stress (ie decreasing the heart rate, slowing the breathing and reducing blood pressure). It can help when learning new physical techniques and is also an aid to imagery.

Performers should try a variety of relaxation techniques to identify the most appropriate technique for them and their sport. There are two main categories:

- **Mind to muscle techniques** focus on reducing worry and clearing the mind, which in turn results in decreases in muscular tension. Examples include:
  - thought stopping, where negative thoughts are prevented from entering the mind by concentrating on pleasant ones
  - breathing exercises (eg centring) which help to calm and relax the body
  - autogenic relaxation where self-talk produces physical sensations of warmth and heaviness

  - meditation (relaxation) which slows the metabolism and calms the mind without the spiritual commitment (ie counting sheep to promote sleep, repeating a mantra).

- **Muscle to mind techniques** concentrate on reducing muscular tension, which in turn has a calming effect on the mind. The most commonly used technique is progressive muscular relaxation (PMR) in which performers systematically tense and relax muscle groups throughout the body. This action releases muscular tension and helps to relax the body completely.

Coaches should familiarise themselves with various relaxation techniques and recognise when performers can make use of them. Deep relaxation techniques are ideal for helping performers sleep the night before a competition, particularly when the performer is anxious about the forthcoming event. However, deep relaxation should not be used immediately before an event because of the negative effects of becoming too relaxed before performing (optimal arousal and performance, see Section 2.4 on Page 48).

Routines

These refer to the patterns of behaviour or rituals adopted by performers prior to competition and before specific events within the competition (eg before set pieces in games, prior to the start of a race, before executing a throw or shooting). They are valuable because they enable performers to follow a set pattern of behaviour at a time when increased arousal and perhaps anxiety may interfere with preparation. In addition they ensure that attention is correctly and positively focused, the benefits of imagery can be incorporated and confidence can be raised through following a familiar routine. It is often used by basketball players at the free throw line, tennis players prior to serving, sprinters preparing to leave the blocks and gymnasts before each event. It can also be used to provide some structure in the 24-hour period before a big competition.

Typical Routine for Swimmer

Night before:
- familiarisation with accommodation, pool environment, eating facility
- pool session (light if in taper phase) with emphasis on starts and turns, racing techniques, pace work and long swim-down
- relaxation and massage
- meal – good carbohydrate and fluid intake
- relaxation and imagery session
- warm shower and good night's sleep.

Morning of event:
- good breakfast with plenty of fluids at least two hours before event
- team meeting or personal time for relaxation
- travel time.

At event:
- general warm-up including 15 mins stretching work, 45–60 mins swim
- warm shower and change into dry warm clothes
- structured time away from pool side during which watch some events, observe the starter
- 35–40 mins before event prepare for race – 25 mins stretching/pulse raising with relaxation and imagery, working through race plan
- ten mins before start to pool side – goggles and hat on early, general focusing and relaxation, imagery of start and first turn
- to blocks – slowly remove outer clothing (often in a set order) in last 30 secs, sit on block or stand behind focusing on lane and imagery of start and first turn, deep breathing to relax.

Thought Stopping

This is a technique for replacing negative self-talk and replacing it with positive statements. Performers learn to recognise quickly the small voice inside the head (eg 'What if I serve a double? What if I miss? What if I lose? I can't play at all today. Don't drop this one again') and use a trigger word such as *stop* or *change* to break the downward spiral of thoughts. Positive self statements (sometimes referred to as affirmations) are then used in place of the negative statements so refocusing attention onto the positive aspects of performance with the associated benefits of reducing anxiety, improving concentration and restoring confidence.

SUMMARY

Mental training techniques can help performers sustain and enhance their commitment, self-confidence and concentration; and maintain appropriate emotional control to reduce the negative effects of anxiety. Common mental training techniques in use in sport include:

- goal setting to help performers progress along the performance highway – enabling them to learn new techniques and experience success regularly as they attain their long term goals

- imagery which can help performers improve concentration, gain emotional control, gain confidence and enhance the development and execution of skills

- thought stopping and positive self-talk which help to eliminate negative self-talk so focusing attention on the here and now, reducing the effects of excessive anxiety and self doubt

- relaxation to help performers create their optimal physical and mental state. It tends to facilitate the effectiveness of other mental skills (eg imagery, concentration techniques) and can enhance the execution of skills – both during learning and competition

- the use of routines to prepare for competition and for specific situations.

Coaches should help performers to develop and practise these mental training techniques and the benefits they offer, and should give them an opportunity to practise using them.

2.6 Training Strategies

A great deal can be done in training to develop mental skills and prepare for the psychological pressures of competition. Although mental skills such as imagery and centring can be learnt initially away from the sports arena, they must soon be implemented into coaching sessions and practised alongside the practical sports skills and in realistic situations. Coaches should devise a range of situations to achieve this – structured sessions, mock competitions, competition training strategies as well as prior to and during the actual competition.

Through this form of training, it is possible to introduce competition variables in a controlled way so performers gradually learn strategies to cope with the sort of situations they may need to face – the effects of the audience, disappointments and errors, unfavourable officiating decisions and verbal abuse. They learn to be able to employ the specific mental skills to enable them to concentrate, retain and build confidence, and cope with anxiety whatever the situation.

Tape-recorded audience and competition noise can be introduced into this form of training particularly where performance is judged subjectively and the audience can influence both the performer and the judges (eg artistic gymnastics, ice dancing, highboard diving and kata routines in karate). However, there are some negative aspects to competition training. It can desensitise performers to the competitive situation to the extent that performers may lose the benefits (the positive gains from physical and psychological arousal) they gain from the competitive situation itself. There is a potential trade-off so competition training should be used appropriately.

A competition training routine for gymnasts could start with a prolonged warm-up followed by the judging routines. The time for the warm-up can be gradually reduced to the four minutes allowed in actual competition. Once the warm-up is completed, gymnasts could be required to sit quietly before their turn during which time they can use concentration and imagery strategies to ensure their focus of attention is on the performance. The gymnasts could then carry out their routines and wait until after the session has ended before receiving any feedback. This process mirrors the situation at competitive gymnastic events.

What if scenarios can also be used to prepare for every eventuality.

What if:

- I false start
- I fall off the beam
- I run the first lap too fast
- the match goes to extra time
- a key player gets injured
- the audience only supports my opponent?

For each one, it is possible not just to plan the best solution but also to practise coping with that in the midst of the physical stress of training or the psychological pressure of a mock competition.

TASK

Think of at least four common distractions that affect you when participating in sport.

What training strategies can you use to help overcome these distractions in the future?

2.7 On the Day

One of the coach's most important roles on the day of a competition is to ensure performers are prepared physically and mentally and that everything runs smoothly. Most of the background work for the day of competition should already have been completed – however, many unexpected events may take place and an appropriate word from the coach can help the performers to remain focused and on target for achieving their goal.

It is especially important that coaches say and do the right thing at the right time. This includes:

- ensuring performers carry out an adequate and effective mental as well as physical warm-up and cool-down
- providing the right information – not too much, for performers will be quickly overloaded with information, not too unfamiliar – last minute changes may not be the best ploy
- providing constructive, positive and useful feedback whenever appropriate or possible
- providing an appropriate calm and confident role model – remember that non-verbal communication is readily picked up by performers.

Mental Warm-up

Performers should warm-up mentally while they prepare their bodies physically for competition. Mental warm-ups help to focus attention on the goals and relevant cues, optimise physical state and enhance self-confidence. When a skill is performed initially, it requires a number of trials before the appropriate technique is established successfully. Mentally rehearsing a movement prior to performing can enhance the skill by pre-tuning the muscle and nerve impulses to promote effective and efficient action.

The content of a mental warm-up will vary depending upon the performer, the sport and the environment. However, it might include a form of relaxation to enable performers to reduce the effects of anxiety, self-talk to increase their self-confidence and imagery to prepare the body and mind for the forthcoming action.

TASK

In most sports, performers have an opportunity to warm-up before competing (eg tennis players have a knock-up; golfers and gymnasts have practice sessions). However, in some sports a warm-up decrement occurs and can present a serious problem. In gymnastics for example, following a two minute warm-up, gymnasts may have to wait for up to 40 minutes before they are required to perform technically difficult and often dangerous routines. Mental training techniques (eg attention control, imagery) can greatly help in these situations by focusing the gymnast's attention on the forthcoming performance and initiating the movement patterns required.

What happens in your sport?

Do you allow your performers time to have a mental warm-up?

If your sport permits substitution, how well are players prepared mentally to join the game?

What to Say and What Not to Say

It is rare for two performers equal in every aspect to react in the same way to the same situation. Each individual responds differently depending on the perceived importance of a given event. Some performers like to congregate and talk while others sit quietly alone to prepare. Some performers feel apprehension or worry and scan the environment for cues to help them cope. Inevitably, they seek reassurance and positive direction from the coach and team mates. In certain sports (eg judo, rugby, shooting and athletics), the performers have to handle these problems on their own because the coach is not allowed contact with them during the competition.

sports coach UK

In other sports, the coach has regular opportunities to talk to performers and can influence their level of motivation, concentration and decision making (eg gymnastics, basketball).

The coach should encourage performers to use their mental skills to:

- manage any anxiety they may be experiencing
- focus attention on the task or agreed goal
- visualise themselves successfully achieving the goal
- mentally rehearse the task
- talk positively to enhance their self-confidence.

Part of the art or skill of coaching is knowing what to say and when to say it. The only way coaches can decide if it is appropriate to offer advice or guidance is by knowing their performers well through a good working relationship. This will enable them to decide whether or not it is appropriate to offer advice or support on the competition day.

The important role the coach plays during competition is shown in the following case study of a gymnast suffering from competitive anxiety.

On the day of competition the coach realised the importance of not being too critical and concentrated on observing performance only. However, in previous training sessions the coach was always enthusiastic and forthright with comments. The gymnast interpreted this competition silence as the coach being annoyed and critical of the performance. This increased the gymnast's anxiety which resulted in a poor performance relative to previous performances. Eventually this problem was overcome.

After the competitive event, it is important to cool-down mentally as well as physically. Many coaches provide feedback but only limited performance analysis immediately after the competition. It is better to wait a few days (or at least hours) before engaging in the more detailed analysis – to identify the good and not so good aspects of performance and develop training goals and programmes for future improvement. The initial mental cool-down helps the mental recuperation (ie cope with the aftermath of the competition stress, the disappointments, the frustrations, the elation).

2.8 Summary

This chapter has focused on psychological preparation for performance by examining the four Cs – ways of raising self-confidence, reducing the negative effects of anxiety (control), focusing attention and maintaining concentration, and increasing commitment.

Appropriate goal setting can be one of the most effective methods of enhancing self-confidence both in the short and long term. Understanding the complex relationship between stress or anxiety and performance should sensitise coaches to the need to treat each performer as a unique individual – different ways of learning, assessing demand and coping with stress.

Certain mental skills will suit some performers better than others – the coach's job is to help the performer learn to prepare for and cope with the pressures of competition. This takes time and should be an ongoing part of the training and competition programme.

Recommended Reading

There are several sources of further reading which you may find useful:

Bull, S.J., Albinson, J.G. and Shambrook, C.J. (1996) *The Mental Game Plan: Getting Psyched for Sport.* Eastbourne: Sports Dynamics. ISBN: 0-951954-32-6.

Hardy, L. and Graham Jones, J.(1994) *Stress and Performance in Sport.* London: John Wiley & Sons. ISBN: 0-471934-876-9. *(Out of Print)*

Moran, A. (1996) *The Psychology of Sport Performers: A Cognitive Analysis.* Hove: Psychology Press. ISBN: 0-863774-43-1.

Morris, T. (1995) *Sports Psychology – Theory, Applications and Issues.* Brisbane: John Wiley & Sons. ISBN: 0-471335-49-5.

Sellars, C. (1996) *Mental Skills: An Introduction for Sports Coaches.* Leeds: **sports coach UK**. ISBN: 0-947850-34-1.*

Nideffer, R.M. (1992) *Psyched to win.* Champaign, IL: Leisure Press. ISBN: 0-880114-63-0.

Orlick, T. (1990) *In Pursuit of Excellence.* Champaign, IL: Human Kinetics. ISBN 0-880114-80-4.

You are also recommended to the following **scUK** workshops/resources (see pages 68–70 for further details):

– *Building Self-Confidence*
– *Goal-setting and Planning*
– *Handling Pressure*
– *Improving Concentration*
– *Imagery Training*

* Available from Coachwise 1st4sport (tel 0113-201 5555 or visit www.1st4sport.com)

TASK

In your next coaching session identify one performer who wishes to improve his/her mental skills and carry out the following exercise:

Use the table below to rate and monitor the performer's stress level at various times before, during and after a competitive event. Plot the results on a graph to help identify the key periods where stress significantly affected the performer.

One week prior to competition	1	2	3	4	5	6	7	8	9	10
One day prior to competition	1	2	3	4	5	6	7	8	9	10
One hour prior to competition	1	2	3	4	5	6	7	8	9	10
During competition	1	2	3	4	5	6	7	8	9	10
Immediately after competition	1	2	3	4	5	6	7	8	9	10
One day after competition	1	2	3	4	5	6	7	8	9	10

(Scale 1 = not anxious, 10 = highly anxious).

Ask the performer to explain what he/she feels at the key times before, during and after competition when the stress level rises (ie cannot concentrate, poor coordination, butterflies, tension). Encourage the performer to classify each feeling as either beneficial or detrimental to performance.

Use this information and the information from the graph to devise a mental training programme which counters any negative affects of anxiety and helps improve the performer's ability to focus attention and remain self-confident before, during and after a competitive event.

CONCLUSION

This handbook offers guidance to coaches, performers and students on how to apply psychology to improve motivation, mental toughness and sports performance.

Where Next?

To help put some of the ideas into practice, you are strongly recommended to go back and reread the summary panels throughout the text and work through the tasks at the end of each chapter. Where appropriate, you should follow up references offered at the end of each chapter.

To continue to update and develop your coaching knowledge and skills, you are advised to take note of the workshops and resources recommended throughout the book. These will help to extend your knowledge further on specific topics and improve your coaching.

Recommended **scUK** workshops and resources (complimentary with the corresponding workshop) include:

scUK Develop Your Coaching Workshop	Accompanying Resource
A Guide to Mentoring Sports Coaches	A Guide to Mentoring Sports Coaches
Analysing your Coaching	Analysing your Coaching
Coaching and the Law	–
Coaching Children and Young People	Coaching Young Performers
Coaching Disabled Performers	Coaching Disabled Performers
Coaching Methods and Communication	The Successful Coach: guidelines for coaching practice
Creating a Safe Coaching Environment	Creating a Safe Coaching Environment
Equity in Your Coaching	Equity in Your Coaching
Field-based Fitness Testing	Field-based Fitness Testing
Fitness and Training	Physiology and Performance
Fuelling Performers	Fuelling Performers
Goal-setting and Planning	A Guide to Planning Coaching Programmes
Good Practice and Child Protection	Protecting Children

scUK Develop Your Coaching Workshop	Accompanying Resource
Imagery Training	Imagery Training
Improving Practices and Skill	Improving Practices and Skill
Injury Prevention and Management	Sports Injury: prevention and first aid management
Motivation and Mental Toughness	Motivation and Mental Toughness
Observation, Analysis and Video	Observation, Analysis and Video
Performance Profiling	Performance Profiling
The Responsible Sports Coach	–
Understanding Eating Disorders	–

If you need more information on basic mental skills and qualities, you are recommended to work through the **scUK** home study pack *An Introduction to Mental Skills.*

For further details on specific and advanced areas, you are also recommended to the following **scUK** resources:

– *Building Self-confidence*
– *Handling Pressure*
– *Improving Concentration*

Details of all **scUK** resources are available from:

Coachwise 1st4sport
Coachwise Ltd
Chelsea Close
Off Amberley Road
Armley
Leeds LS12 4HP
Tel: 0113-201 5555
Fax: 0113-231 9606
Email: enquiries@1st4sport.com
Website: www.1st4sport.com

scUK also produces a technical journal, *coaching edge*, formerly known as *Faster, Higher, Stronger (FHS)*. Details of this service are available from:

sports coach UK
114 Cardigan Road
Headingley
Leeds LS6 3BJ
Tel: 0113-274 4802
Fax: 0113-275 5019
Email: coaching@sportscoachuk.org
Website: www.sportscoachuk.org

For subscription information regarding *coaching edge* and back copies of *FHS* please telephone 0113-290 7612.

For further details of **scUK** workshops being run in your area, contact the **scUK** Business Support Centre (BSC) or log on to www.sportscoach.org/improve/workshop/search.asp

sports coach UK Business Support Centre
Sports Development Centre
Loughborough University
Loughborough
Leicestershire LE11 3TU

Tel: 01509-226130
Fax: 01509-226134

Email: bsc@sportscoachuk.org

Useful Contacts

The British Association of Sport and Exercise Sciences
Leeds Metropolitan University
Carnegie Faculty of Sport and Education
Fairfax Hall
Headingley Campus, Beckett Park
Leeds LS6 3QS
Tel: 0113-283 6162
Fax:0113-283 6162
Website: www.bases.org.uk

The British Psychological Society
St Andrews House
48 Princess Road East
Leicester
LE1 7DR
Tel: 0116-254 9568
Fax: 0116-247 0787
Website: www.bps.org.uk

Notes

Notes